SCOTTISH STEAM ALBUM

BRIAN MORRISON

AMBERLEY

The 1.30 pm (Saturdays only) Greenock Princes Pier to Glasgow St. Enoch train passes the Princes Pier engine sheds on a hot June day in 1957. In charge is a rather grimy Pickersgill Class 3P 4—4—0 No. 54468 from Hamilton depot (66C).

First published 2022

Amberley Publishing
The Hill, Stroud
Gloucestershire, GL5 4EP

www.amberley-books.com

British Library Cataloguing in Publication Data.
A catalogue record for this book is available from the British Library.

ISBN 978 1 4456 9980 6 (print)
ISBN 978 1 4456 9981 3 (ebook)

Typeset in 10pt on 13pt Sabon.
Typesetting by SJmagic DESIGN SERVICES, India.
Printed in the UK.

Contents

Introduction

The overnight train from Kings Cross pulled into Edinburgh Waverley station early on a Saturday morning in May. The sun was already shining quite brightly and the activity that could be observed from the carriage window included a number of locomotive types that I had not previously had the opportunity to photograph.

Although having returned to Scotland quite often this was to be the first of many occasions that a week's holiday north of the border was to be spent pursuing my then new found interest of railway photography.

It was 1952. Dieselisation hadn't been heard of. The name Beeching meant nothing to the railwayman or to the enthusiast. There were still services to most parts of the country and, of course, steam was everywhere!

Even before alighting from the train I had taken two photographs from the carriage window; a Class J88 0—6—0T shunter acting as station pilot and a Class D34 4—4—0, with the lovely Scottish name of *Glen Fintaig*, arriving with a local service from Berwick-upon-Tweed.

Not possessing a car in those days my journeyings were all by rail but, with the judicious use of a current Bradshaw timetable, I was able to travel quite extensively around the country and, that first year, obtained photographs at Perth, Aviemore, Forres, Gollanfield, Inverness, Strathcarron, Kyle of Lochalsh, Keith, Aberdeen, Dunfermline and, of course, Edinburgh.

Many of the locomotive types at work in Scotland never ventured south of the Border and I tried, not only to obtain good photographs of Scottish trains, but to record an example of every locomotive class that existed there at that time. In fact the quest was not to be completed until Spring 1958 when I eventually managed to hunt down an example of the post-grouping development of the old Caledonian Railway 439 Class 0—4—4T in Glasgow St Enoch station.

This album includes at least one example of every type of steam locomotive to be seen only in Scotland during the decade of the 1950s except for one or two that had already seen the cutting torch before I had managed to track them down. It is arranged to take the reader from Edinburgh up the East coast via Dunfermline and Thornton Junction to Dundee and Aberdeen, thence across to Inverness and Kyle of Lochalsh and back South through Aviemore, Perth, Stirling and Glasgow to Kilmarnock and Dumfries with quite a few stops on the way. My visits were usually made in late May or early June of each year and, for the most part, were blessed with good weather conditions.

I still holiday in Scotland every year and, on occasions, have the added bonus of a business visit. Photographic activities are, however, mainly restricted to the current diesel and electric scene. Although there is nothing like the diversity of motive power that there was in the 1950s and many of the lines have been axed there is, for me, still a considerable interest in the Scottish railway scene and now, with the use of a car, I have been able to visit some lines and photograph from some locations that were impossible for me in the circumstances that prevailed twenty years before.

Brian Morrison
SIDCUP, KENT.

Edinburgh Waverley

A Class J83 0—6—0T No. 68477 waits impatiently for the right away with empty coaching stock. Built in 1900-1 the 4 locomotives that made up the class were designed by Holmes for the North British Railway and originally designated as Class D.

An early morning commuters' train from Berwick-upon-Tweed arrives at its destination behind Gresley Class VI 2—6—2T No. 67659. Although calling at all stations the service was still timed at under the hour.

Emerging into the sunshine from Calton Tunnel, a local service from North Berwick arrives at Waverley station headed by ex-North British Class D34 4-4-0 No. 62490 *Glen Fintaig*. Designed by Reid, the original 32 locomotives of the type were built between 1913-20 and given classification 'K'. No. 256 *Glen Douglas* has been preserved in original NBR livery.

With just a two-coach engineers' inspection train to pull Gresley Class A3 Pacific No. 60068 *Sir Visto* is certainly not overtaxed!

Gresley Class A3 Pacific No. 60041 *Salmon Trout* and Class V2 No. 60825 simmer gently outside Edinburgh Waverley awaiting their next turn of duty. At the time that this photograph was taken — July 1953 — both these engines were allocated to Edinburgh; the V2 to St. Margaret's (64A) and the Pacific to Haymarket (64B).

Recently outshopped after a major overhaul and repaint, ex-North British Class J83 0—6—0T No. 68474 was one of the Waverley station pilots when photographed in May 1952.

The Gresley Class A4 Pacifics allocated to Haymarket were always well turned out in the 1950's and No. 60004 *William Whitelaw* was no exception when captured pulling away from Waverley with the 'Elizabethan' express for London, King's Cross.

Class D1 1/2 4-4-0 No. 62672 *Baron of Bradwardine* waits in a siding outside Waverley station, having brought in a local service from Berwick. These locomotives were a post-grouping development of the original Great Central 'Directors' class built to the Scottish loading gauge and with long-travel valves. Known as 'Improved Directors' 12 were constructed by Kitsons and 12 by Armstrong Whitworth to add to the original 11 built four years earlier in 1929 by Robinson for the G.C.R.

The four-coach local service for Ladybank is moved away on time from Edinburgh Waverley at 3.43 pm headed by 'Shire' Class D49/1 4—4—0 No. 62713 *Aberdeenshire*.

An early morning express for Newcastle is eased away from Waverley by Gresley Class A4 Pacific No. 60009 *Union of South Africa*, one of the class that has been preserved.

Former North British 'Scott' Class D30 4-4-0 No. 62424 *Claverhouse* runs light past the castle walls at Edinburgh in 1953. Designed by Reid and constructed between 1912-20 all 27 engines were named after characters from the novels of Sir Walter Scott and included such marvellous examples as *Hal o' the Wynd, Laird o' Monkbarns, Black Duncan* and *Wandering Willie*.

The 9.50 am from Aberdeen upon arrival at Edinburgh Waverley behind Class A2 Pacific No. 60529 *Pearl Diver*, one of the class fitted with a double blast pipe and multiple valve regulator. The 'sawn off' stovepipe chimney did nothing for the locomotive's appearance.

The local stopping train from Edinburgh Waverley to Larbert stops at Haymarket station, in the Edinburgh outskirts, on a dull June afternoon in 1952. 'Hunt' Class D49/2 4-4-0 No. 62743 *The Cleveland* is in charge. This locomotive and No. 62744 *The Holderness* were the only two 'Hunts' ever allocated to Scottish sheds.

'Improved Director' Class D11/2 No. 62692 *Allan-Bane* rests outside Hay market depot; one of 10 of the class allocated to 64B.

Haymarket Motive Power Depot (64B)

Right: A diminutive Reid ex-North British Class J88 0—6—0T No. 68328 acts as shed pilot. Built between 1905-19 the 35 engines that made up the class were originally designated as North British Class F.

Below: 'Scott' Class D30 4-4-0 No. 62437 *Adam Woodcock* receives minor attention outside Haymarket shed between duties on the Edinburgh — North Berwick local service.

Above: A. number of 'Shire' Class D49/1 4—4—0's were allocated to sheds across the border and the Haymarket share was five including No. 62719 *Peeblesshire*.

Left: The impressive front end of Peppercorn Class A1 Pacific No. 60159 *Bonnie Dundee* backing on to the Haymarket turntable.

Above: Holmes ex-North British Class J36 0—6—0 No. 65235 *Gough* moves away from the Haymarket coaling tower after a refill. Although dating from 1888 it was two of this class that survived to become the last steam locomotives of British Rail to remain at work in Scotland in 1967.

Below: A number of the Class J36 engines saw service overseas during the First World War and, upon their return to British shores, received commemorative names painted upon the splashers: practically the only examples of the ubiquitous 0—6—0's in Great Britain to be so honoured. A recently repainted *Gough* contrasts with the weatherbeaten and practically unreadable works plate.

Above and below: Scores of compound engine oil drums form the foreground to Class A1 Pacific No. 60160 *Auld Reekie* pictured outside Haymarket shed. Always one of my favourite Scottish nameplates, wouldn't this one look fine adorning a present-day British Rail diesel!

Passing St. Margaret's

Right: With a guard's van and rake of empty coaching stock, Reid ex-North British Class N15/1 0-6-2T No. 69152 struggles up the gradient past St. Margaret's, Edinburgh.

Below: Thompson Class B1 4—6—0 No. 61244 passes St. Margaret's with a semi-fast for Edinburgh.

St. Margaret's Motive Power Depot — Edinburgh (64A)

Above and opposite above: Two entirely dissimilar Reid designs for the North British Railway photographed at Edinburgh St. Margaret's in 1952. Heading the page is Class N15/1 0—6—2T No. 69186 dating from 1924 when the design was perpetuated by the L.N.E.R. and below one of his Class J88 0—6—0T's No. 68338, constructed a few years earlier and bearing the early style of B.R. identification, making the turntable look much larger than was really the case.

Opposite middle: Running 'light engine' past St. Margaret's shed, a very well-kept Gresley Class V3 2—6—2T No. 67624 fairly glints in the evening sunshine. This class was a development of the Glass VI 2—6—2T's introduced from 1930. The final ten engines of the 92 strong class were built with a 200 lb per sq. inch boiler and classified V3 and many of the V1's were similarly dealt with when their original 180 lb. per sq. inch boilers became life expired, this locomotive being numbered among them.

Former Caledonian Railway 'Pug' Class OF 0—4—OST No. 56035 poses for the camera on a misty June morning in 1953. Note the permanently attached wooden tender.

Another of the St Margaret's Class J88 0—6—0's. No. 68334 awaits an exit from the shed yard which can, in this case, only be made by crossing the turntable which is in use.

Although similar to the Caledonian 0—4—0ST opposite, No. 68102 has a North British parentage and was designed by Holmes and dates from before the turn of the century. In North British days the locomotive was of Class G but became L.N.E.R. Class Y9 from 1923.

Class N15 0—6—2T No. 69173 at St Margaret's in 1955. Sixty-nine of this class were inherited by the L.N.E.R. at the 1923 grouping and they proceeded to build another 30 to Reid's North British design.

Above: With a cosy looking tender cab to combat Scottish winters, ex-North British Class J35/4 0—6—0 No. 64479 receives a grilling under a hot June sun in the St Margaret's yards.

Right: Looking rather incongruous without the middle pair of driving wheels, Gresley Class J38 No. 65927 awaits their return at St Margaret's in 1957. The locomotive had been rebuilt with a Class J39 boiler.

Stanier Class 5MT 4—6—0 No. 45180 approaches the Forth Bridge crossing with the 3.10 pm Perth —Edinburgh express.

Dunfermline

Above and opposite: The 3.50 pm train to Inverkeithing prepares to leave Dunfermline Lower station behind 'Scott' Class D30/2 4—4—0 No. 62441 *Black Duncan*. Heading the opposite page an unlikely combination of Class VI 2-6-2T No. 67610 piloted by Class J37 0—6—0 No. 64556 head ten very mixed bogies away from Dunfermline and head for the direction of Edinburgh. From the opposite direction Class B1 4—6—0 No. 61132 races by with the 1.54 pm Edinburgh — Aberdeen express.

Above: Gresley Class A3 Pacific No. 60076 *Galopin* takes the incline away from Dunfermline in fine style with the 3.05 pm Edinburgh — Perth express.

Below: *Pearl Diver* is caught by the camera again passing Dunfermline with the afternoon Aberdeen — Edinburgh express.

Right: The Reid North British Class J37 0—6—0's were designed principally for freight operation. During the summer months, however, they were sometimes brought into use for passenger and excursion traffic. Here a seven-coach load is depicted north of Dunfermline with a service that did not appear in the working timetables of the time. The locomotive is No. 64565.

Below: A local service for Edinburgh heads south from Dunfermline behind Class V3 2—6—2T No. 67672.

By now the diversity of motive power to be seen at Dunfermline will have been apparent to the reader. Adding to the types already depicted is 'Improved Director' Class D11/2 4—4—0 No. 62676 *Jonathan Oldbuck* steaming strongly against the grade with the 10.35 am Edinburgh — Perth service.

Stanier 'Black Five' 4—6—0 No. 45043 heads past Dunfermline towards Edinburgh in the Spring of 1953 with some rather mixed empty coaching stock.

Gresley ex-Great Northern Class K2 2—6—0 No. 61741 draws to a halt at Dunfermline Lower station with a train from Anstruther to Glasgow and optimistically carries an express headlamp code.

Guards van sandwich! Class J35 0—6—0's Nos. 64475 and 64476, both allocated to Dunfermline shed (62C), head away from home towards the north with this unusual 'load'.

With a ten-coach load Reid North British Class J37 0–6–0 No. 64558 passes Dunfermline with a summer excursion.

The 'Prize Length' of permanent way north of the station is traversed by Class A2 Pacific No. 60525 *A.H. Peppercorn* heading an express for Edinburgh.

Thornton Junction

Left: Gresley Class D49/1 4—4—0 No. 62718 *Kinrossshire* moves the 2.50 pm local service for Dunfermline Upper away from Thornton Junction station on a beautiful June day in 1957.

Below: A freight heading in the direction of Dundee passes Thornton Junction hauled by J37 0—6—0 No. 64577 of Edinburgh St Margaret's.

A Fort William (65J) based Stanier 'Black Five' No. 44973 strangely heads the 12.46 pm Dundee Tay Bridge — Edinburgh Waverley semi-fast shown at Thornton Junction in the summer of 1957.

A North British 'Glen' Class D34 4—4—0 No. 62488 *Glen Aladale* prepares to leave Thornton Junction with the branch train to Crail. In the background is McIntosh Class 2P 0—4—4T No. 55217 engaged on shunting duties.

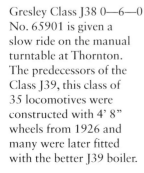

Gresley Class J38 0—6—0 No. 65901 is given a slow ride on the manual turntable at Thornton. The predecessors of the Class J39, this class of 35 locomotives were constructed with 4' 8" wheels from 1926 and many were later fitted with the better J39 boiler.

Worsdell ex-North Eastern Class J72 0—6—0T No. 69013 outside Thornton Junction shed (62A). This quite remarkable class was first introduced in 1898. Ten further engines were built by the L.N.E.R. in 1925 and a further 25 under the auspices of British Railways between 1949-51 making a grand total of 75. Rightly, one has been preserved — No. 69023 *Joem*.

Inside the Thornton repair shops Class N15/1 No. 69150 and an ex-W.D. 2-8-0 No. 90560 receive attention.

Above and below: Class D49/1 4—4—0 No. 62729 *Rutlandshire* and Class D11/2 4—4—0 No. 62679 Lord Glenallan (above) and Class J38 0—6—0 No. 65907 (below) swelter under a hot sun outside Thornton Junction shed.

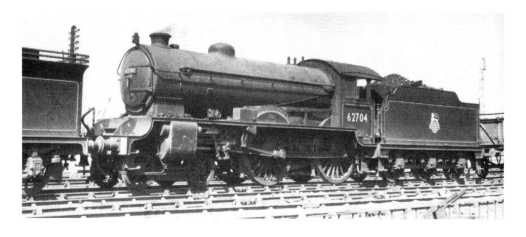

Above and opposite: There was always a great variety of locomotive types to be seen on shed at Thornton Junction. Just five are illustrated on these two pages. 'Hunt' Class D49/2 4—4—0 No. 62744 *The Holderness*, Class N15/1 0—6—2T No. 69143 with the then new B.R. emblem, 'Shire' Class D49/1 4—4—0 No. 62704 *Stirlingshire*, 'Glen' Class D34 4—4—0 No. 62492 *Glen Garvin* and J35/5 0—6—0 No. 64474 being 'fed and watered'.

Above: A down coal train heads northwards from Dundee behind one of the former North British Class J37 0—6—0's No. 64598. Over 100 of these engines were constructed between 1914-21 and they were the largest freight locomotives on the North British system.

Below: 'Scott' Class D30 4—4—0 No. 62438 *Peter Poundtext*, coaled up and ready for the next turn of duty, is photographed in the shed yards at Dundee (Tay Bridge).

Fitted with a spark arrester for use in the docks, ex-North British Y9 0—4—OST No. 68108, takes in the sun at Dundee in 1955.

Coaled and watered and ready to head towards Dundee Tay Bridge station to take out a Tayport branch local for St Andrews, an ex-North British Class C16 4—4—2T No. 67484 waits ahead of Class J37 0—6—0 No. 64587 which has been prepared to haul a Dundee — Carlisle freight.

The placing of headlamps to form the standard express code was a popular joke with Scottish enginemen when concerned with the more mundane duties. An 'express' trip freight moves away from Dundee (Tay Bridge) with Class J83 0—6—0T No. 68466 in charge.

Haymarket-based A3 Pacific No. 60096 *Papyrus* is turned at Dundee ready to make the journey back to Edinburgh.

McIntosh ex-Caledonian Class 3F 0—6—0T No. 56323 shunts the yards at Dundee.

Thompson Class B1 4—6—0 No. 61101 charges the gradient out of Dundee Tay Bridge station with a semi-fast working in May 1958. The engine was the only one of the 409 of the Bl's constructed to be allocated to Dunfermline (62C).

Aberdeen — The Granite City

Scheduled to depart from Aberdeen at 7.10 pm the 'Aberdonian' for London, King's Cross awaits the 'right away' behind Class A2 Pacific No. 60531 *Bahram*, one of the Pacifics allocated to Aberdeen Ferry hill shed, which will take the train as far as Edinburgh Waverley.

Above: Only six Class N14 0—6—2T's were built by the North British in 1909 and only three were left to be taken into B.R. stock in 1948. By 1953, when this photograph was taken, No. 69125 was the last of the class and due to be withdrawn at any time. The old lady, in quite good external condition at least, passes Aberdeen with an empty stock working early one July morning.

Below: Still with the legend 'N.E.' on the tender Gresley Class J39/2 0—6—0 No. 64795 backs onto a freight at Aberdeen later on the same day.

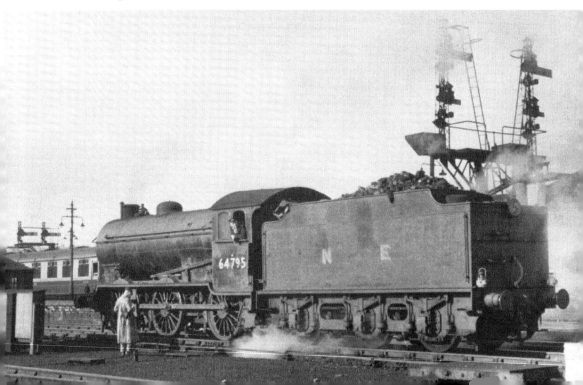

Above: Having been released from the platform after departure of the stock that it had brought in earlier, Class C16 4—4—2T No. 67496 gallops back to Ferryhill sidings for the next load.

Below: A misty morning sun has little to highlight on the rather grimy exterior of Class K2 Mogul No. 61782 *Loch Eil* hauling a freight for Montrose away from Aberdeen.

Above: B.R. Standard Class 4MT 2—6—4T No. 80004 makes a spirited getaway from Aberdeen with the 6.33 pm local service to Fraserburgh. Making eleven stops before reaching its destination the train was timed to arrive at 8.14 pm.

Below: Reid North British Class N15/2 0—6—2T No. 69128 acts as station pilot above the Aberdeen rooftops just outside the station.

Above: A late evening freight from Kittybrewster to Arbroath runs round the outside of Aberdeen station headed by tender first Class J35/4 0—6—0 No. 64482. There was no discernible external difference between the J35/4 and the J35/5 but underneath, so to speak, the part 4's had slide valves and the part 5's piston valves.

Below: Pictured at the Aberdeen buffer-stops Class K2/2 2-6-0 No. 61782 has just arrived with the 4.59 pm ex Ballater.

A pair of Stanier 'Black Fives' head the up 'Saint Mungo' from Aberdeen to Glasgow Queen Street. Timed to depart at 9.35 am this was a very popular service and the combined power of Nos. 44957 and 44669 will have been very necessary before the 14 well-laden coaches reach their destination.

Gresley Class J39/3 0—6—0 No. 64975 heads an up freight bound for Dundee through platform 7 at Aberdeen. The Class J39/1 was matched with a 3,500 gallon tender, the J39/2 had a 4,200 gallon type and the J39/3 were fitted with a variety of N.E. tenders; the type shown here was a 4,125 gallon kind.

Just 30 Class C15 4—4—2T's were constructed by the North British between 1911-13 to Reid's design. All survived to be taken into B.R. stock in 1948 and the last was not withdrawn until 1961. No. 67455 completes watering up just outside Aberdeen in 1952 whilst engaged upon station pilot duties.

Holden ex-Great Eastern Class B12/1 4-6-0 No. 61502 prepares to depart with the 6.10 pm Aberdeen — Keith train on a wet May evening in 1953. Twenty-five of this class were exiled to Scotland from 1931 by the L.N.E.R. and this particular engine was one of the last survivors. Unlike its English counterparts, No. 61502 retained an original Belpaire boiler to the end.

The 9.50 am Aberdeen — Edinburgh draws away from the station behind Class A2 Pacific No. 60528 *Tudor Minstrel*.

Two morning expresses head south away from Aberdeen, both with a Stanier 'Black Five' at the helm. On the left is No. 44967 heading for Glasgow and on the right No. 44995 making the run to Perth.

Manning Wardle ex-Great North of Scotland Class Z4 0—4—2T No. 68190 rests at Waterloo Quay, Aberdeen, while the crew have a morning tea break between shunting and marshalling operations. Built in 1915, specifically for use in the Aberdeen Docks, the original class of four locomotives were later sub-divided into classes Z4 and Z5.

Dawn at Ferryhill, Aberdeen. Gresley Class V4 2—6—2 No. 61701 moves away with the 6.25 am freight for Laurencekirk. Only two of the class were ever built, with the first of them receiving the name Bantam Cock. It was, of course, inevitable that the other loco would be unofficially christened *Bantam Hen*! On the right is J39/3 0—6—0 No. 64975 engaged on marshalling.

An early morning train from Ballater arrives at Aberdeen behind Gresley ex-Great Northern Class K2/2 Mogul No. 61783 *Loch Shell*. Those of this class allocated to Scottish sheds were all fitted with a side window cab to afford a little winter comfort to the crews.

Above: Engaged upon shunting duties in the yards just west of Aberdeen station is Class C16 4—4—2T No. 67501.

Below: Just outside the station, bunker first Class N14 0—6—2T No. 69125 arrives with a trip freight from Montrose.

Above: Another view of Class V4 2—6—2 No. 61701 setting off from Aberdeen with the 6.25 am freight for Laurencekirk. A trip to Aberdeen was made specially in 1957 to obtain a photograph of this class. To succeed with the quest it was necessary to get out of bed in the small hours, as on the previous evening the locomotive was tucked in a dark corner of Ferryhill shed. Scottish air at this hour is very bracing!

Below: Pickersgill ex-Great North of Scotland Class D40 4—4—0 No. 62278 *Hatton Castle* moves an up freight away from Aberdeen yards in 1952. This was one of the class built by Heywood in 1920 with superheater.

Passing Ferryhill

Above: Peppercorn Class A2 Pacific No. 60531 *Bahram* storms past Ferryhill, south of Aberdeen, with the 5.17 pm to Edinburgh.

Opposite bottom: Allocated to Aberdeen Ferryhill (61B) *Blue Peter* was kept as standby engine for a number of years and was only used when the necessity arose. A hot box on the rostered locomotive brought the Thompson Class A2 Pacific into use on the up 'Aberdonian' on 25 June 1957 and here No. 60532 rounds the Ferryhill curve past the locomotive depot with the Granite City's most famous train. *Blue Peter* has, of course, been preserved and the scene here, could again be reproduced. A very pleasant thought.

Holmes North British Class J36 0—6—0 No. 65297 rounds the curve at Ferryhill heading for Montrose with a freight from Inverurie.

Taking the incline out of Aberdeen in grand style Stanier Class 5MT 4—6—0 No. 44703 steams southwards past Ferryhill with the 5.25 pm express for Glasgow Queen Street via Perth.

Ferryhill Motive Power Depot — Aberdeen (6IB)

Above and opposite: During the 1950's Ferryhill Shed accommodated no less than 14 different classes of locomotive. In addition types from other sheds were always coming and going and the variety to be seen at any one time was sometimes quite surprising. Class N15/2 0—6—2T No. 69128, one of the classes allocated there, is shown outside the shed and Class J37 0—6—0 No. 64630, a visitor from Dunfermline (62C), was photographed in the yards.

Opposite below: In excellent external condition and retaining a Midland style chimney, Class 2P 4—4—0 No. 40614 is a surprise visitor to Ferryhill from Dumfries (68B).

Above: Glasgow St. Rollox (65B) ex-Caledonian 'Jumbo' Class 2F 0—6—0 No. 57253 has been coaled and watered and waits to return south.

Below: The handsome lines of Gresley Class V4 2-6-2 No. 61701 are shown to advantage at this angle. Although constructed for the West Highland line both engines of the class were based at Ferryhill during the 1950's and, in fact, finished their days at Thornton Junction working local goods and the very occasional passenger turn.

Kittybrewster

An up van train from Peterhead passes Kittybrewster heading for Aberdeen behind Class B1 4-6-0 No. 61350, one of the class fitted with a self-cleaning smokebox as indicated by the letters 'SC' on the smokebox door.

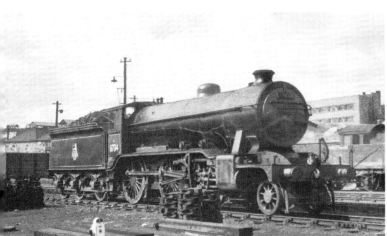

Above: Running tender first into Kittybrewster yards with a freight from Keith, Class D40 4-4-0 No. 62278 *Hatton Castle* is pictured on one of its last workings before withdrawal.

Left: One of the Scottish based ex-Great Northern Class K2 Moguls No. 61734, from Keith shed (61C), poses for the camera in the yards at Kittybrewster before returning north with a freight.

Awaiting the last journey. Great North of Scotland Class D40 4—4—0 No. 62264 had already been officially withdrawn when discovered amid the coaches and trucks in Kittybrewster yards and was soon to be broken up.

Kittybrewster Motive Power Depot — Aberdeen (61A)

Worsdell ex-Great Eastern Class F4 2—4—2T No. 67157 has been retired for the night inside the shed at Kittybrewster. One hundred and sixty of this class were constructed for the Great Eastern between 1884–1909 but, when this photograph was taken, only four survived with this locomotive being the last left on Scottish soil. At the time I was annoyed that I was unable to take a proper record of the engine inside the shed but, with the passage of time, it is now realised that this is superior to a standard locomotive portrait.

Above: One of the Scottish-based Class K2/2 2—6—0's with side window cab, No. 61793 is turned before making its way back north with a pick-up goods.

Left: Eight of the 17 'Glen' Class D34 4—4—0's were allocated to Kittybrewster. One of them, No. 62479 *Glen Sheil*, simmers under a hot June sun awaiting the next call of duty.

There being no workings at the Waterloo Quay, Aberdeen, on Sundays the little Z4 and Z5 dock tanks could normally be seen on shed at Kittybrewster where they were all based. Tucked into a dark corner of the depot are Nos. 68191, 68192 and 68190.

Above: With the words 'Boiler Empty' chalked on the tank side, Manning-Wardle ex-Great North of Scotland Class Z5 0—4—2T No. 68192 has been hauled out into the sunshine specially for the camera. They were always a very co-operative lot at Kittybrewster!

Below: On another occasion the camera captures one of the two Class Z4 0—4—2T's No. 68191. This class was a little smaller and a little less powerful than the Class Z5's. They had 3'6" driving wheels as against ones of 4', weighed 5 tons less at 25 tons 17 cwt and had a tractive effort of 10,945 lb.

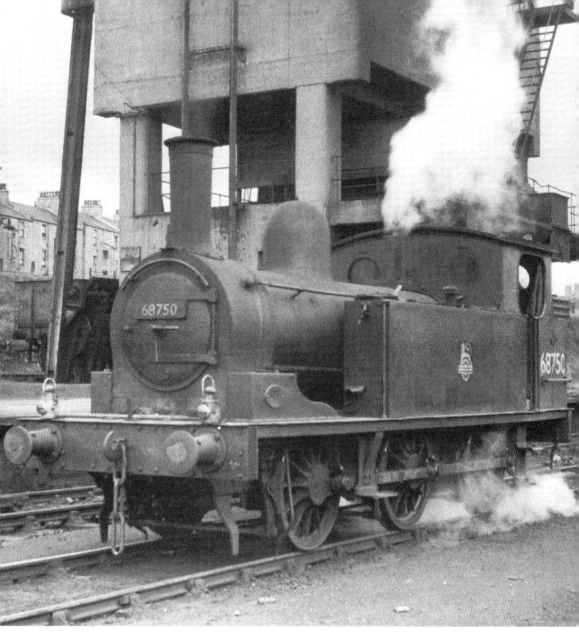

Above: W. Worsdell's North Eastern Class El 0—6—0T's became Class J72 when the railway was absorbed by the L.N.E.R. in 1923. By the 1950's a dozen of the class were at work north of the border including No. 68750 allocated to 61A seen here rattling past the coaling tower engaged upon shed pilot duties. Note, once again, the express headcode!

Opposite above: Engaged upon truck marshalling in the Kittybrewster yards a Reid North British Class N15/2 0—6—2T No. 69129 is paused while a photograph is taken of the shunter who salutes the camera! Although there were 99 locomotives of Class N15 there were only six in part 4 of the class and these were the originals dating from 1910 that were a development of the Class N14 Cowlairs Bankers.

Opposite below: The 12.20 pm semi-fast from Keith to Aberdeen approaches Inverurie headed by Thompson Class B1 4—6—0 No. 61400.

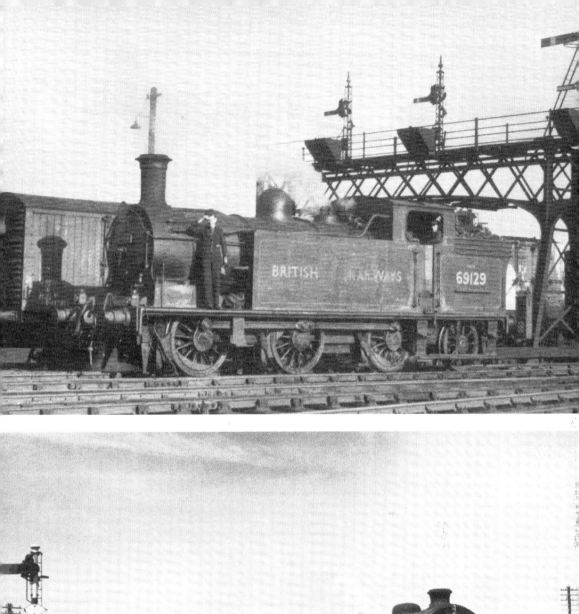

Inverurie

Above, left and opposite above: 'Scott' Class J30 4—4—0 No. 62418 *The Pirate*, a McIntosh ex-Caledonian 0—4—4T No. 55236 and a Reid ex-North British Class J37 0—6—0 No. 64621 all receive attention inside the works at Inverurie in 1957. The photograph at the foot of the opposite page of Class N15/1 0—6—2T No. 69186 shows how a finished product looked.

The 9.25 am Elgin — Aberdeen service via Buckie and Portsoy and the 9.30 am between the same two stations but via Craigellachie and Keith joined up at the exchange station known as Cairnie Junction. Class B1 No. 61324 has come off the 9.30 am portion and all six coaches are taken on to their destination by No. 61343 of the same class.

Cairnie Junction

Fresh from Inverurie Works, Pickersgill ex-Caledonian Class 3P 4—4—0 No. 54507 passes through Cairnie Junction being tested out 'light engine' before being returned to its home shed Dumfries (68B).

Keith

Above and right: During the decade of the 1950's the acknowledged 'home' of the Great North of Scotland Class D40 4—4—0's was Keith (61C). No. 62264 is pictured outside the depot, with the nameplate of No. 62275 *Sir David Stewart* being taken from inside, its owner being inaccessible to the camera at the time.

Pickersgill Caledonian Class 3P 4—4—0 No. 54473 shunts wagons in the sidings at Elgin before moving away with a freight for Inverness.

Elgin

Above and right: Before withdrawal, and subsequent renovation and preservation, Class D40 4—4—0 No. 62277 *Gordon Highlander* was still a most handsome machine despite its coating of honest dirt. Having deposited wagons it had brought in from Boat of Garten the locomotive was to take over yard shunting for a while. Chatting with the driver he informed me that he had heard rumours that 'The Highlander' was to be preserved. As things transpired the rumours were perfectly true and a fine job was completed on the ex-Great North of Scotland engine a few years later. Even new cast nameplates were provided in lieu of the painted type it carried here.

Forres

Above and left: Whilst waiting for the 10.52 am train for Keith to leave Forres I managed these two photographs, one from each side, of former Caledonian 4—4—0 No. 54471 which was rostered for the turn. The old Caledonian 72, 113, 139 and 928 classes were all very similar and this engine belonged to the latter section, although classified merely as 3P by the L.M.S. and by British Railways.

Above: The 10.50 am
Perth — Inverness
express headed
by Stanier 5MT
4—6—0 No. 44991
photographed from
the carriage window at
Forres.

Right: The passing
of the ways at
Gollanfield. From the
same carriage window
another Stanier 'Black
Five' is caught by the
camera hauling an up
ballast train.

Inverness — Capital of the Highlands

Left: Pickersgill ex-Caledonian 72 Class 3P 4—4—0 No. 54480 prepares to leave Inverness in 1953 with an engineers' inspection train for the north.

Below and opposite: 'Black Fives' in profusion. No. 44975 waits to leave Inverness with the morning train for Kyle of Lochalsh. No. 44979 pulls away with the other morning departure for the north — the 9.15 am to Tain and Nos. 44788 and 44961 are harnessed and draw slowly away with the 'Royal Highlander' for London, Euston.

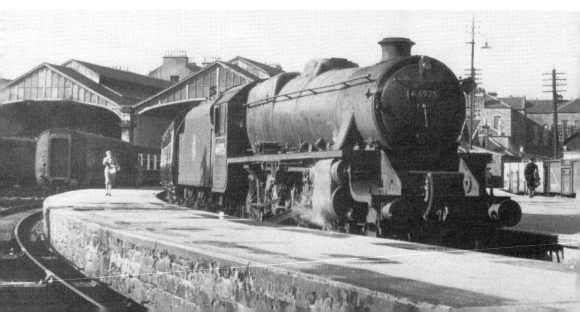

The up 'Royal Highlander' for London, Euston snakes away from Inverness headed by Stanier 'Black Five' 4—6—0 No. 44961 which is piloted by sister engine No. 44788.

On a sunny June evening in 1956 the Inverness yards are marshalled by McIntosh ex-Caledonian Class 3F 0—6—0 No. 56293 which has not had its appearance in any way enhanced by replacing the original Caledonian chimney with one of the ugly stovepipe variety.

Drummond ex-Highland Class IP 0—4—4T No. 55053 undergoes repair inside the works in 1957. The last examples of the Highland Railway to remain in normal service the two engines of the class were retained to work the branch from Dornoch to The Mound and were eventually withdrawn in the year that this photograph was taken.

Lochgorm
Works — Inverness

Right: Four years earlier, in 1953, McIntosh Caledonian Class 2P 0—4—4T No. 55218 receives attention at the same spot. Note the Caledonian chimney and how better the locomotive on the opposite page would have looked with such an adornment.

Below: Acting as works shunter at Lochgorm is former Caledonian 'Pug' 0—4—0ST No. 56011. Thirty-nine of these little engines were constructed between 1878–1908 and 14 survived into B.R. days, with the last being withdrawn in 1962.

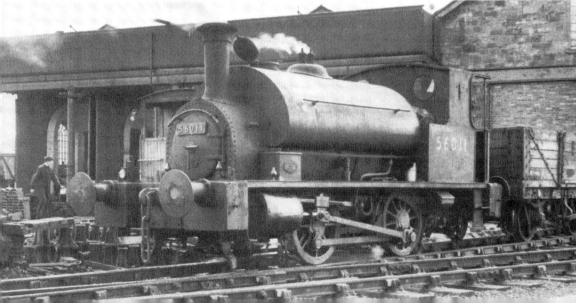

Wandering around outside the Works late one summer evening in 1953 I came across a most unexpected sight. Officially withdrawn from service some months before I thought I had missed the opportunity to capture on film a P. Drummond ex-Highland 'Small Ben' 4—4—0. But there before me was No. 54398 *Ben Alder*, which I learned later was scheduled for preservation. In fact, the engine was later broken up. Some say by accident, others by design.

Above and left: Ben Alder was one of 20 of the class built around the turn of the century and was one of just three to receive a British Railways number in 1948. It would have made a very fine addition to the National Collection, but it was not to be.

Inverness Motive Power Depot (60A)

Above and overleaf: Inverness was another of the many sheds in Scotland that invariably contained a great variety of motive power, from Stanier 'Black Fives' to diminutive 0—4—0 dock tanks, many of the classes being survivors of the 1923 Grouping. Depicted on these two pages are Class OF 0—4—0ST No. 56038, Class 3F 0—6—0T No. 56291, Class 3F 0—6—0T No. 57642 (one of the Caledonian 652 class) and 3P 4—4—0 No. 54480.

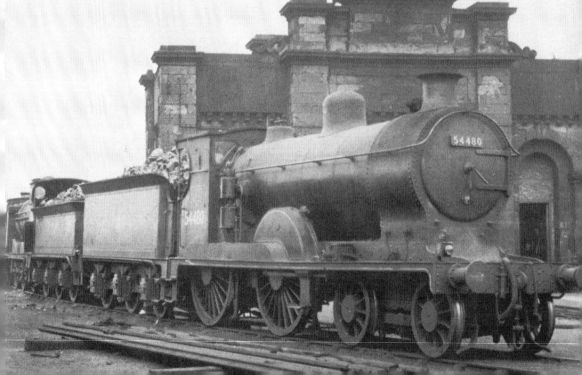

Above: Just a coach destination board. But what pictures it conjured up.

Below: The passing of the ways at Strathcarron. The train on which I am travelling to Kyle of Lochalsh passes the 10.45 am from Kyle to Inverness headed by Stanier 4—6—0 No. 44998. Timed to arrive at the Highland capital at 2.24 pm the train is scheduled to make 14 stops before its destination including some at romantic sounding places such as Duncraig, Achnashellach, Achnasheen, Lochluichart and Dingwall.

Kyle of Lochlash

Left: With the Skye landmass shrouded in mist behind it, ex-Caledonian Class 2P 0—4—4T No. 55216 shunts the yards at Kyle in pouring rain.

Below: The 9.05 am from Inverness arrives at Kyle behind the inevitable 'Black Five'. 4—6—0 No. 44722 was one of the 15 of the class allocated to Inverness at this time.

Culloden Moor

Above left, above right and right: An Inverness — Perth semi-fast evening service heads across the moors into the setting sun behind Stanier Class 5M 4—6—0 No. 45360. On the opposite page No. 45469 of the same class heads south with another semi-fast service earlier on the same day and, from the other direction, ex-Caledonian Class 3P 4—4—0 No. 54466 drifts downhill with the 2.48 pm from Aviemore to Inverness.

Above: Between Culloden Moor and Daviot, the heavy 5.15 pm Inverness — Euston sleeper is moved southwards at a fair pace behind a pair of Stanier 'Black Fives'. The train engine is No. 44698 and the pilot No. 44979.

Left: The 9.25 am Edinburgh Princes St. — Inverness express sets away from Aviemore after the obligatory stop. Having already slogged over Druimuachdar summit the two 'Black Fives' Nos. 45459 and 45165 will still need all of their combined power to combat Slochd summit which has yet to come before their destination is reached.

Stanier 4—6—0 No. 45125 from Perth (63A) marshalls trucks in the yards at Blair Atholl before returning south with a pick-up freight that will eventually terminate at Stirling.

Perth

Right: B.R. Standard
Class 5MT 4—6—0 No.
73152, one of the class
with Caprotti valve gear,
draws empty stock away
from Perth station whilst
engaged upon station pilot
duty.

Below: Even the
professionals are
sometimes wrong! With
'Class D34' clearly painted
on the buffer beam, No.
62436 *Lord Glenvarloch*
is, in fact, a Class D30/2
4—4—0 and is pictured
here making the prescribed
stop at Perth with the 9.35
am from Edinburgh.

Gresley Class A3 Pacific No. 60043 *Brown Jack* pounds away from Perth with seven somewhat mixed bogies that make up a semi-fast for Edinburgh Waverley. On the left Jubilee 4—6—0 No. 45692 *Cyclops* can be seen proceeding towards the station to take out a van train for Forfar and Arbroath.

An unusual combination at the southern end of Perth station in 1953. Stanier Class 5 No. 44931 pilots Fairburn Class 4MT 2—6—4T No. 42272 with a three-coach stopping train for Stirling; the tank is working back to Dairy Road shed (64C) after overhaul in Perth Works.

A Rangers Football Club special approaches Perth on the way to Aberdeen headed by B.R. Standard Class 5MT 4—6—0 No. 73154, another of the class fitted with Caprotti valve gear.

The 8.03 am Ladybank — Perth approaches journey's end in 1954 behind Thompson Class B1 4—6—0 No. 61358. Awaiting a clear road with a southbound fish train is Hughes Class 5MT 2—6—0 No. 42746 from Glasgow St. Rollox (65B).

Jubilee 4—6—0 No. 45715 *Invincible* gathers speed past the Perth coaling tower with an express working for Manchester.

McIntosh former Caledonian '29' Class 3F 0—6—0 No. 56331 on shunting duty in the Perth yards. Built between 1895–1922 this class of locomotives and the '782' type were grouped together under the one class heading and to all intents and purposes had the same specifications. One hundred and forty seven were built in all and the whole of them came into B.R. stock upon Nationalisation in 1948 with the last being withdrawn in 1962.

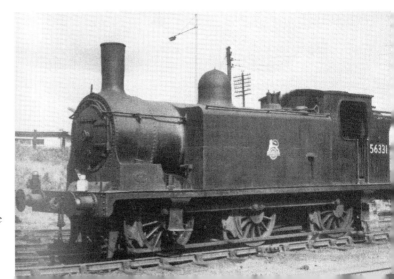

Above, below and opposite above: Being an individual who is reluctant to go to bed and even more reluctant to arise it was something of a minor miracle for me to be out on the lineside at Perth just after dawn! In fact, my hotel overlooked the station and I was awoken by the quite considerable activity that was going on in the early morning light. Sounds of various locomotives pervaded my ears until, in the end, I could stand the frustration no more and decided to spend an hour with the camera before breakfast. I was not disappointed as the three examples of the morning's work illustrated on these two pages will testify. The first movement was that of the station shunter, a McIntosh ex-Caledonian Class 2P 0—4—4T No. 55213, arranging a gaggle of vans into proper order. Soon afterwards came J 38 Class 0—6—0 No. 65900 with a freight for Aberdeen and, with the sky beginning to cloud up, a long haul of trucks came up in the other direction hauled by WD 2—8—0 No. 90705 heading for Thornton Junction. Breakfast tasted particularly good that morning.

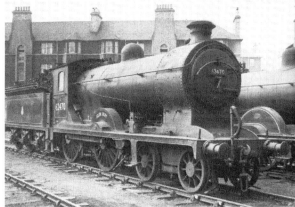

Right: Reid North British Class D34 4—4—0 No. 62470 *Glen Roy* was a Perth engine for a number of years.

Below: Former L.M.S. Class 4F 0—6—0 No. 44318 and No. 44315 of the same class 'on shed' at 63A in 1955. Although there were 580 of these locomotives constructed, they were never a common sight in Scotland as only 25 of them were allocated to sheds across the border.

Perth Motive Power Depot (63A)

A Dugald Drummond Caledonian Class 2F 0—6—0 No. 57473 at Perth in 1952 still retains the condensing apparatus originally fitted for the Glasgow low level lines.

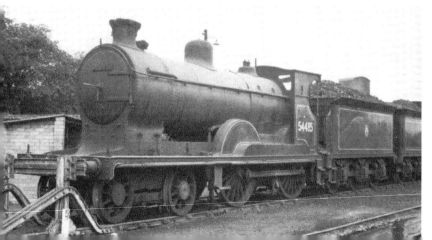

With the chimney covering showing that the locomotive is in store, No. 54485 is one of the Pickersgill former Caledonian '72' Class 3P 4—4—0's allocated to Perth.

Gresley Class J38
0—6—0 No. 65923 is
a visitor to Perth from
Dunfermline (62C).

With the distinctive
Reid North British cab,
a Class J37 0—6—0
No. 64566 has been
prepared to take a
return freight working
south to Edinburgh,
and backs out of
the Perth shed yards
after reversal on the
turntable.

A visitor to Perth
from Stirling (63B),
Reid North British
Class J35/4 0—6—0
No. 64520 has been
overhauled and
repainted in the works
and will shortly return
south with a freight.

Drummond 'Jumbo' Class 2F 0—6—0 No. 57384 photographed in the Perth shed yards in 1957. Two hundred and forty-four of this class were constructed between 1883–97 making them, numerically, the largest on the Caledonian system. They all came into L.M.S. ownership in 1923 and all but six survived to receive a British Railways number. This particular example has been fitted with an L.M.S. boiler.

Left: Thompson Class B1 4—6—0 No. 61348 from Aberdeen Kittybrewster (61A) backs off Perth shed in 1953 to be made ready for a return north with a semi-fast working. Pulling away from the yards on the left is an ex-Great North of Scotland Class D40 4—4—0 No. 62271 with a down freight.

Below: Introduced by Holmes for the North British from 1888, Class J36 0—6—0 No. 65243 *Maude*, seen here in Perth yards, has been preserved by the Scottish Railway Preservation Society at Falkirk. Recently outshopped when this photograph was taken the name had not been returned to the left-side splasher but was still to be seen on the right-side one!

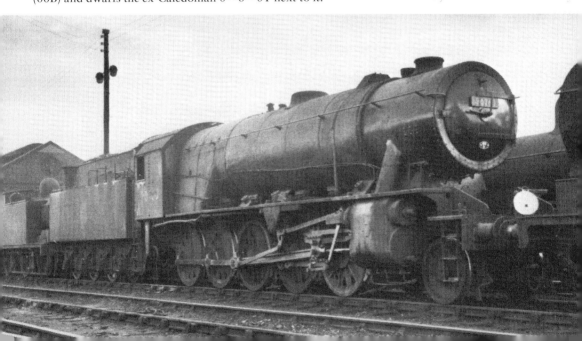

Above: The McIntosh '92' Class 2P 0—4—4T's were introduced to the Caledonian at the turn of the nineteenth century for use on the Glasgow Central low level lines and were all built with condensers as can be seen on No. 55126 shunting empty stock at Stirling. Although 19 of the original total of 22 survived to B.R. days, inroads were soon made into them and when this photograph was taken in 1957 this was the sole survivor of the class.

Below: One of the mighty ex-War Department 2—10—0's, No. 90760, rests at Motherwell shed (66B) and dwarfs the ex-Caledonian 0—6—0T next to it.

Top, above and left: Kipps, a small subshed to Glasgow Eastfield, always had an interesting variety of motive power on view. Just three of the types that could be seen are depicted here. Permanently attached to a wooden tender is Holmes North British Class Y9 0—4—0ST No. 68117. Class J36 0—6—0 No. 65214 contrasts nicely with another of the same class No. 65285 with cut down boiler mountings.

Glasgow Termini

Above left, above right and below: At Glasgow Central 'Princess Coronation' Class 8P Pacific No. 46235 *City of Birmingham* has been appropriately rostered to haul the 9.25 am express to Birmingham New Street. At the top of the opposite page a 'Royal Scot' 4—6—0 No. 46117 *Welsh Guardsman*, its grimy exterior trying vainly to reflect the rays of the setting sun, waits to pull out of Glasgow St. Enoch with the 8 pm 'Starlight Special' for Marylebone. Opposite, a Stanier 'Black Five' 4—6—0 No. 44677 moves away from Glasgow Buchanan Street at the head of the 7.35 pm Sunday express for Aberdeen.

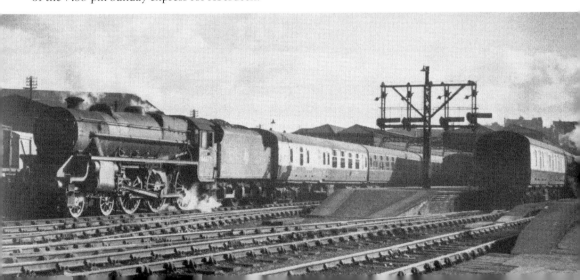

Above and left: Just a few of the locomotives that were under repair in St. Rollox Works in June 1957 — 'Jumbo' Class 2F 0—6—0 No. 57364, No. 57446 of the same class, 'Jubilee' 4—6—0 No. 45732 Sanspareil, McIntosh Class 3F 0—6—0 No. 57601, B.R. Standard Class 5MT 4—6—0 No. 73005, B.R. Standard Class 3MT 2—6—0 No. 77015 and 'Black Five' No. 44795.

St. Rollox Works — Glasgow

This profile of B.R. Standard Class 5MT 4—6—0 No. 73148 on the turntable at St. Rollox clearly shows the Caprotti valve gear that just 43 of the 172-strong class had fitted. One example, No. 73129, has been preserved.

St. Rollox Motive Power Depot (65B)

Above: Back on St. Rollox shed after overhaul and repaint in the Works are McIntosh ex-Caledonian '29' Class 3F 0—6—0T No. 56336 and a 'Crab' Mogul No. 42837.

Left: A Reid North British Class J88 0—6—0T No. 68326 shunts the yards at Glasgow Eastfield in 1955. Constructed between 1905–19 as North British Class 'F' the 35 locomotives of the class survived the 1923 grouping and Nationalisation in 1948 without loss. The first of the class was, in fact, withdrawn in 1954 and the last in 1962.

Eastfield Motive Power Depot — Glasgow (65A)

Holmes North British Class J36 0—6—0 No. 65258 fitted with condensing apparatus has a well-filled tender preparatory to departing south for Carlisle with a goods. Five of the 96 locomotives remaining in this class by the middle 1950's were allocated to Eastfield but, in fact, No. 65258 was one of the 10 from Edinburgh St. Margaret's (64A).

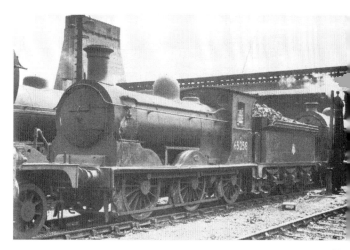

Engaged upon shunting 'dead' locomotives about the large Eastfield shed complex is another Holmes North British design, a Class J83 0—6—0T No. 68447.

Above, left and bottom:
The locomotive
allocation at Glasgow
Eastfield was
particularly diverse.
Illustrated here are
Class C16 4—4—2T
No. 67485, Class K2/2
2—6—0 No. 61774
Loch Garry and Class
J37 0—6—0 No. 64633.

Above and right: In 1937 six Gresley-designed locomotives for the West Highland line emerged from Darlington Works. Classified K4, they had identical cylinders and motion to the K3 Moguls that were completed at Darlington in the same year. All were allocated to Eastfield for the majority of their lives although one, rebuilt by Thompson in 1945 with two cylinders and reclassified as Kl/1, was retained by the small Fort William shed (65J). No. 61994 The Great Marquess photographed in 1957 has been preserved in original L.N.E.R. passenger green livery.

Above, left and bottom: A few more of the myriad locomotive types on display at Glasgow Eastfield. Former WD 2—10—0 No. 90770 in a line-up that includes Gresley Great Northern Class J50/3 0—6—0T 68957 and North British Class J37 0—6—0 No. 64627; Class J36 No. 65315 fitted with condensing apparatus and ex-North British Class C15 4—4—0 No. 67460 alongside a Class N15 0—6—2T and backing onto an ex-works condition Class 2P 4—4—0 No. 40623.

A close-up of the Kitchener nameplate
which includes the famous badge of the
Royal Engineers.

The most unexpected sight at 65A on a day in June 1957 was one of the War Department
2-10-0s which had not been taken into B.R. stock, No. 601 Kitchener from the Longmoor
Military Railway. The locomotive had been internally modified by the North British Locomotive
Company in a number of ways, and under an agreement with the Ministry of Supply it was
tested for a time between Carlisle and Hurlford using the L.M.R. No. 3 Dynamometer Car and
the Mobile Test Units. Painted in blue with large headlight and Westinghouse brakes, the engine
was a notable contrast to the normal work-stained condition of the B.R. members of the fleet, as
can be seen by the example of the same class on the page opposite. With Kitchener here are Class
J50/3 0-6-0T No. 68956 and Class C16 4-4-2T No. 67485.

Cowlairs Works — Glasgow

Left: Undergoing heavy repair inside Cowlairs Works are Reid Class J88 0—6—0T No. 68354 from Polmont (64E) and Class B1 4—6—0 No. 61340 from Eastfield (65A).

Below: In Cowlairs Works yards awaiting its turn for attention is Gresley Class K2/1 2—6—0 No. 61729, one of only three of this type to be fitted with a side window cab.

Inside Cowlairs on the same day is Gresley Class J38 0—6—0 No. 65905 completely stripped of all cab fitments and controls and without wheels. The relatively small jacks look hardly strong enough to hold a locomotive weighing nearly 59 tons.

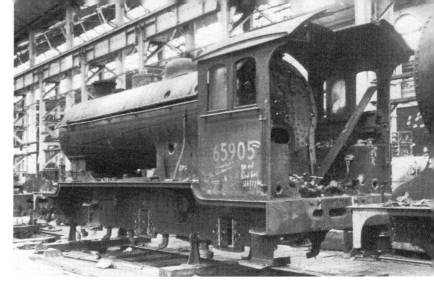

In the sidings at Larkfield busily engaged upon carriage shunting is Pickersgill ex-Caledonian Class 2P 0—4—4T No. 55237. Specially designed for banking duties and introduced in 1922 all four engines that made up the class were fitted with special cast-iron front buffer beams. During their Caledonian days they were known as Class '431'.

British Railways Standard Class 6MT Pacific No. 72003 *Clan Fraser* pulls away from the Glasgow Polmadie yards with a freight bound for Stirling. Just 10 of these small Pacifics were built at Derby in 1952 for service on the Scottish Region and all were named after famous clans. Half of the class were allocated to Polmadie (66A) and the other half to Carlisle Kingmoor (68A).

Above: A haul of iron piping is taken through Polmadie by 'Black Five' 4—6—0 No. 44668, one of the class fitted with Skefco roller bearings on the driving coupled axle.

Below: Fitted with an unglamorous stovepipe chimney is former Caledonian 'Jumbo' 0—6—0 No. 57243 resting outside Polmadie sheds after bringing in a freight from its home shed at Stirling (63B).

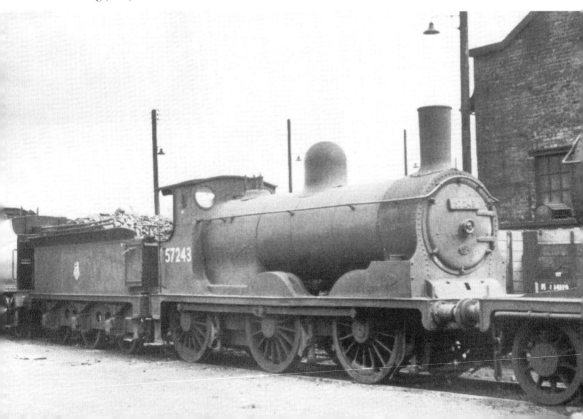

Above and below: The B.R. Standard 'Britannia' Class 7MT Pacifics that were initially allocated to Scotland all received names that were appropriate. No. 70054, the last of the class, was christened Dornoch Firth and is seen here beside Caledonian '439' Class 2P 0—4—4T No. 55167 which is in store. This practice followed on from that of the old L.N.E.R. who gave Scottish names to many of their Pacifics that were given a home north of the Border — an example of which is the nameplate of Class A2/1 No. 60510 *Robert the Bruce*.

Polmadie Motive Power Depot — Glasgow (66A)

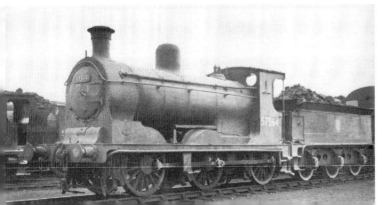

Top, middle and bottom: Glasgow Polmadie was a very cosmopolitan shed, housing as it did, most of the freight engine types that worked in and around Glasgow in addition to the much larger and powerful passenger types both from Scotland and from south of the Border. Former Caledonian dock shunter Class 2F 0—6—0T No. 56153 is in the shed yards together with No. 55239, one of the Caledonian '431' Class 2P 0—4—4T's that retained its original chimney, and Caledonian '812' Class 3F 0—6—0 No. 57564.

Top, middle and bottom: About to return south with an express for London is 'Princess Royal' Class 8P Pacific No. 46212 *Duchess of Kent* while, along the tracks a little way, is 'Jubilee' Class 6P 4—6—0 No. 45665 *Lord Rutherford of Nelson* that was allocated to Glasgow Corkerhill (67A). Inside its somewhat cramped Polmadie quarters is B.R. Standard Class 3MT Mogul No. 77008, one of just two of the class of 15 allocated here.

Marshalling empty stock to form a train for Glasgow St. Enoch at Greenock Princes Pier is Pickersgill ex-Caledonian '928' Class 3P 4—4—0 No. 54468.

Greenock Princes Pier

Above: The 12.40 pm (Saturdays only) from Glasgow St. Enoch arrives at Greenock Princes Pier behind Fairburn Class 4MT 2—6—4T No. 42247.

Right: No. 42190 of the same class moves slowly away from the Princes Pier buffer stops with the 2.20 pm for St. Enoch.

Greenock Princes Pier
Motive Power Depot

McIntosh former Caledonian '498' Class 2F No. 56165 rattles past Princes Pier shed yard heading for some refreshment, in the shape of coal and water, after having been actively engaged for a long hot morning in wagon shunting.

Although Princes Pier shed was merely a sub to Greenock Ladyburn (66D) and carried no official shed coding, the allocation of locomotives at any one time was often in excess of the parent depot. Here Pickersgill '72' Class 3P 4—4—0 No. 54506 stands under a very hot June sun with the casing, literally, too hot to touch with the hand. I found out the hard way!

Greenock Ladyburn Motive Power Depot (66D)

Right: Former Caledonian 'Pug' 0-4-0ST No. 56031 and 'Jumbo' 0—6—0 No. 57268 share the shed yard in 1957. The 0—6—0 is one of those fitted with an L.M.S. boiler.

Below: No. 56173 hardly resembles No. 56165 on the opposite page but, in fact, is of the same class. It just shows the difference that the original Caledonian chimney made in a locomotive's appearance.

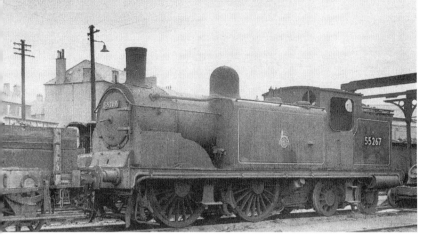

Constructed by the L.M.S. in 1925, No. 55267 was one of a class of 10 engines that were a development of the Caledonian '439' Class 2P 0—4—4T's. This particular locomotive is one of the unfortunates fitted with the dreaded stovepipe.

McIntosh Caledonian '29' Class 3F 0—6—0T No. 56288 and '498' Class 2F 0—6—0T No. 56157 bunker to bunker outside Greenock Ladyburn late on a warm June evening.

With front number and shed plates nicely painted in red and with white smokebox door hinges, a start at least appears to have been made to smarten up this stocky little ex-Caledonian dock shunter No. 56163, by the shed staff at 66D.

Above left: Stanier 'Black Five' 4—6—0 No. 44892 threads a path through Kilmarnock station with a down freight from Carnforth (11A).

Above right: Former L.M.S. Class 2P 4—4—0 No. 40597 moves the four-coach 4.16 pm local train for Glasgow St. Enoch away from Kilmarnock station in 1957. Making stops at all 12 stations on the way arrival time was scheduled for 5.22 pm.

Below: The 3.50 pm express from Glasgow St. Enoch to Dumfries arrives at Kilmarnock — the only stop on the journey — on time at 4.28 pm headed by a dirt encrusted 'Royal Scot' Class 7P 4—6—0 No. 46113 *Cameronian*.

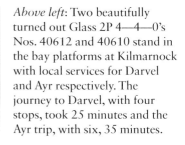

Above left: Two beautifully turned out Glass 2P 4—4—0's Nos. 40612 and 40610 stand in the bay platforms at Kilmarnock with local services for Darvel and Ayr respectively. The journey to Darvel, with four stops, took 25 minutes and the Ayr trip, with six, 35 minutes.

Above right: B.R. Standard Class 5MT 4—6—0 No. 73104 from Corkerhill (67A) leaves Kilmarnock with the 3.08 pm semi-fast to Glasgow St. Enoch from Dumfries.

Middle: 'Royal Scot' Class 7P 4—6—0 No. 46108 *Seaforth Plighlander* darkens the blue sky over Lanarkshire as the very heavy 10.35 am Leeds — Glasgow express is eased away from the down platform at Kilmarnock.

Bottom: A credit to Ayr shed (67C), Class 2P 4—4—0 No. 40610 soaks up the sunshine in the bay platform at Kilmarnock before setting off home with the Saturday 4 pm to Ayr.

Carronbridge

Above, below and right: The old Glasgow & South Western line between Glasgow and Dumfries was always one of photographic interest with a constant stream of traffic during the summer months. Above, an excursion for Heads of Ayr speeds through Carronbridge behind Stanier 'Black Five' 4—6—0 No. 44901 and, on the page opposite, ex-L.M.S. 'Compound' Class 4P 4—4—0 No. 40920 pilots 'Black Five' No. 44995 with a special for Stranraer, and Hughes 'Crab' Mogul No. 42905 heads south with a return excursion to Newcastle.

Dumfries

Left: The 10.58 am from Stranraer arrives at Dumfries behind Class 2P 4—4—0 No. 40616 from Stranraer shed (68C). The 73-mile journey has taken nearly three hours but the line was of a somewhat tortuous nature.

Below: The up 'Thames–Clyde Express' for London, St. Pancras picks up speed again after stopping at Dumfries. The headboard is carried by 'Royal Scot' No. 46103 *Royal Scots Fusilier*.

Right: Class 5MT 2—6—0 No. 42913 restarts from adverse signals with a down freight at Dumfries.

Below: For all that has been said about the ugliness of the stovepipe chimney this one, fitted to 'Patriot' Class 6P 4—6—0 No. 45508, must have been the worst of all.

Dumfries Motive Power Depot (68B)

Above: Stanier Class 3MT 2—6—2T No. 40151 rests between turns at Dumfries shed in 1958. In the background, and giving a good contrast between old and new designs, is an ex-Caledonian 'Jumbo' 0—6—0.

Below: Class 2P 4—4—0 No. 40629, having arrived on a service from Carlisle, waits on shed for the time to return south with the balanced working.

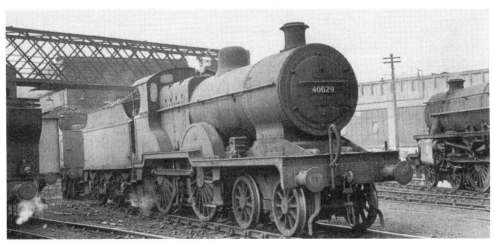

Near Dumfries

Above: Stanier 'Jubilee' Class 6P 4—6—0 No. 45732 *Sanspareil* eases a very long Carlisle — Glasgow freight through Dumfries in the Spring of 1956.

Right: A lightweight goods scurries through the outskirts of Dumfries with 'Crab' 2—6—0 No. 42805 in charge.

Above and below: Taken at the same spot near Dumfries two up freights head southwards headed respectively by B.R Standard Class 5MT 4—6—0 No. 73079 and Hughes 5MT Mogul No. 42884.

Sassenachs!

Designed by Holden for the Great Eastern Railway and constructed in 1911, a batch of Class B12 4-6-0s made their way to Scotland in 1931 and saw out their lives on the Great North of Scotland section. No. 61502 leaves Aberdeen with an evening stopping train for Keith.

Following a number of internal modifications to include superheater elements, blast pipe, arch tubes and brakes, a Riddles War department 2-10-0, No. 601 *Kitchener* of the Longmoor Military Railway in Hampshire, was in Scotland for trials required by the Ministry of Supply. This photograph was taken at Polmadie (66A) and, later the same day, it was 'on shed' at Eastfield (65A). Possibly B.R. Scottish Region were hoping that some of the Army 'bull' would rub off on their cleaners!

Scottish Nameplates

Class D34 4—4—0 No. 62489.

Class D49/1 4—4—0 No. 62725.

Class D30/2 4-4-0 No. 62436.

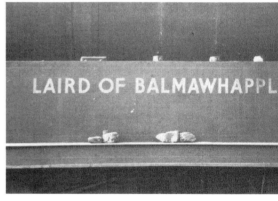

Class D11/2 4—4—0 No. 62691.

Class K2/2 2—6—0 No. 61782.

Class 7MT 4—6—2 'Britannia' No. 70054.

Even a locomotive that had just been through works and been repainted could still be embellished by enthusiastic shed staff. With buffers trimmed with white paint as well as the smokebox door hinges, the shed staff of Hurlford (67B) were, obviously, proud of their charge. Class 2P 4—4—0 No. 40571 was photographed at Greenock at the head of a train for Glasgow.

Ex Works

Despite a day of overcast skies and a steady drizzle the fresh paintwork on ex-L.M.S. Class 2P 0—4—4T No. 55269 brightens the scene at Glasgow St. Enoch quite considerably.

North British Stalwarts

Above and below: Former North British Class J35/4 0—6—0 No. 64530 and J35/5 0—6—0 No. 64476 in charge of freight were photographed at Dundee and Dunfermline respectively. The Reid J35/5 engines were introduced in 1906 with piston valves and the J35/4 variety appeared from 1908 with slide valves.

Titled Trains

The 5.30 pm for Glasgow Buchanan St., the 'Granite City', prepares to depart from Aberdeen behind Stanier 'Black Five' 4—6—0 No. 44980, one of the stud from Perth (63A).

Backing off shed at Aberdeen Ferryhill (61B), Thompson Class A2 Pacific No. 60532 *Blue Peter* has been fitted with the headboard showing it to have been rostered to haul the 7.10 pm 'Aberdonian' for London, King's Cross.

Stanier 'Princess Coronation' Class 8P Pacific No. 46229 *Duchess of Hamilton* on the outskirts of Glasgow with the up 'Caledonian' flyer for London, Euston. This is one of this magnificent class that has been preserved.

Probably the most famous titled train of all time, the 'Flying Scotsman' leaves Edinburgh Waverley just after 10 am on a dull June morning in 1957, hauled by Gresley Class A4 Pacific No. 60019 *Bittern*, just one of this class that has, happily, been preserved.

Scottish Steam Lives On

Above: Preserved Gresley L.N.E.R. Class K4 Mogul No. 3442 *The Great Marquess* prepares to return to Kidderminster and the Severn Valley Railway following a main line test run to Derby on 30th June 1989. Passing the locomotive and entering Derby station is an Intercity 125 High Speed Train forming the 09.22 Penzance–Glasgow Central service, 'The Cornishman'.

Left: Following a spell of main line running in the 1980s, the sole surviving Gresley L.N.E.R. Class D49 4-4-0, No. 246 Morayshire, receives attention by the Scottish Railway Preservation Society at Bo'ness on 30th May 1988.

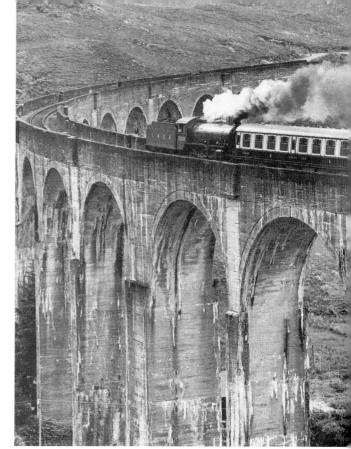

Right: Heading the 13.40 'Royal Scotsman' service from Mallaig to Fort William tender first on 1st June 1988, the sole surviving Thompson L.N.E.R. Class KJ Mogul No. 2005 crosses the reinforced mass concrete arches of Glenfinnan Viaduct, where the 12-chain radius curve of the structure is highlighted in this view taken through a telephoto lens.

Below: This classic view of the 416 yard long Glenfinnan Viaduct surrounded by typical West Highlands' scenery tends to dwarf the six-coach train thereon, as Class K1 No. 2005 hauls the 10.50 Fort William–Mallaig steam excursion on 2nd June 1988.

At the end of a cloudless day Gresley Class A4 Pacific No. 60009 *Union of South Africa* is caught at speed near Blackford, between Perth and Stirling, with the return 'Silver Jubilee Special' to Kircaldy run by the Kircaldy & District Lions Club. Through no fault of the locomotive the train was very late and the sun had already set behind the Glenalmond Hills when this scene was recorded on 28th May 1977.

Situated a few miles west of Edinburgh, the Bo'ness & Kinneil Railway has been the recipient of a number of awards, particularly for its recreated station buildings; the entire line having been constructed on a green field site. On 30th May 1988 ex-National Coal Board, East Fife Area 1954 0-6-0ST Hunslet 3818 No. 19 charges out of the station heading the 16.10 train for Birkhill.

With its light blue Caledonian Railway livery glinting in the low evening sunshine, the Caley 4-2-2 'Single' No. 123 leads L.S.W.R. green Class T9 'Greyhound' 4-4-0 No. 120 near Balcombe, Sussex, on 15th September 1963 with the return 'Blue Belle' special for London Victoria. Now part of the Glasgow Museum of Transport collection. No. 123 is one of a number of preserved locomotives from pre-Grouping Scottish railways which can be viewed in the fine setting of the former Kelvin Hall.

The Forth Centennial

The mighty railway bridge over the Firth of Forth was opened on 4th March 1890. On the same day one hundred years later, a major part of the centenary celebrations was the 'Forth Centennial' special train headed by Gresley Class A4 Pacific No. 60009, renamed *Osprey*, seen here crossing the South Approach Viaduct of the Forth Bridge on the outward run from Edinburgh Waverley.

Above: Having unveiled a commemorative plaque on the South Portal of the bridge, Lord Elgin, Chairman of the Forth Bridge Centenary Trust, and Sir Bob Reid, retiring Chairman of British Rail, are among nearly 300 patrons and guests on the special train, which is seen here returning from Inverkeithing to Edinburgh Waverley over the South Queensferry Cantilever of the Forth Bridge on 4th March 1990.

Left: 'Number Nine' emerges from the Mound tunnel into Princes Street Gardens on 4th March 1990 prior to taking a second 'Forth Centennial' special train from Edinburgh to Perth and back.